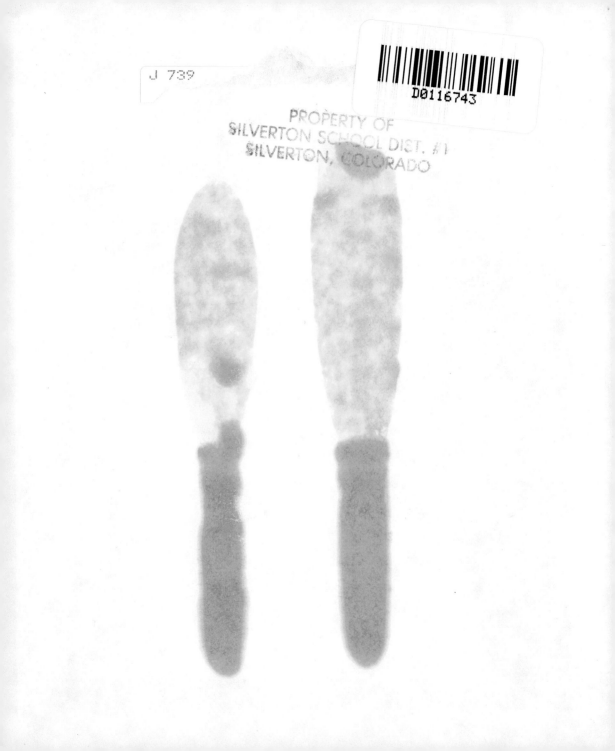

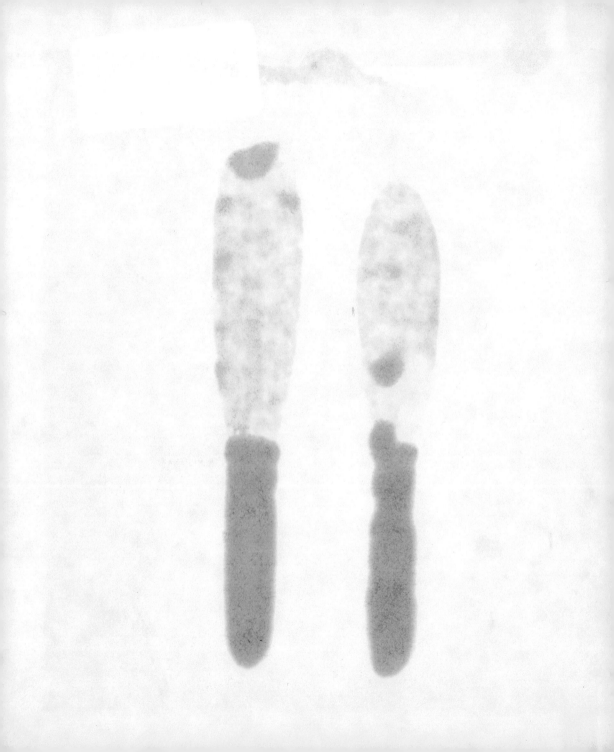

FACT FINDERS
Educational adviser: Arthur Razzell

Armour
Hugh Gregor

Illustrated by Angus McBride and Dick Eastland
Designed by Faulkner/Marks Partnership

Silver Burdett Company

© 1976 Macmillan Education Limited

Published in the United
States by Silver Burdett
Company, Morristown, N.J.
1978 Printing

ISBN 0-382-06238-8

Library of Congress
Catalog Card No. 78-64662

Armour

Ancient Armour

The Ancient Greeks were among the first people to wear armour. A Greek warrior wore armour made of bronze. He carried a short sword, a spear, and a large, round shield.

These Greek soldiers (left), were led by Alexander the Great. They are attacking a Persian army.

Roman Armour

Like the Greeks, Roman soldiers usually fought on foot. They also wore armour on the top half of the body and the legs. In addition to a sword, they carried javelins (spears) for throwing. Their shields were curved to fit round the body.

Legionaries

Standard bearer

Centurion

The Romans liked to watch gladiators fighting. The one on the right is armed only with a trident. He is trying to entangle his opponent in his net. The gladiator on the left wears a helmet. He has armour on one arm and leg.

Roman breastplate

Chain mail

A Norman knight had a shield shaped like a kite. It gave him good protection on horseback. He was covered in a kind of armour called chain mail. He carried a long, heavy sword. The helmet has a piece in front of the nose (called a nasal) to protect the face.

Norman knight

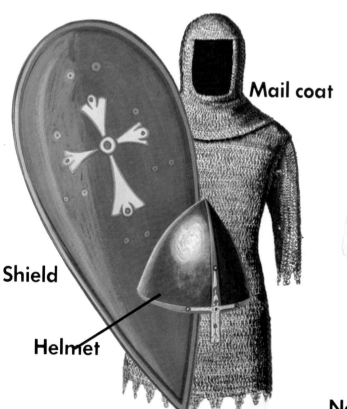

Mail coat

Shield

Helmet

On the right is a close-up view of chain mail. It was made from short pieces of iron bent into rings.

The famous Bayeux Tapestry (below) shows the Normans defeating the English at the Battle of Hastings. Both sides are shown wearing chain mail.

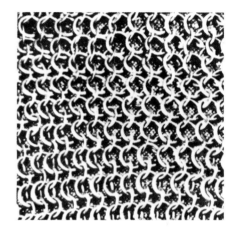

Plate Armour

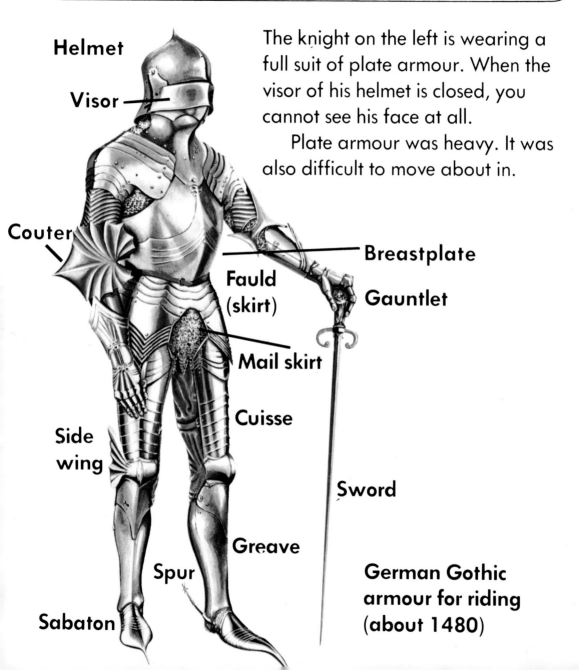

Helmet

Visor

Couter

Side wing

Spur

Sabaton

Breastplate

Fauld (skirt)

Gauntlet

Mail skirt

Cuisse

Sword

Greave

The knight on the left is wearing a full suit of plate armour. When the visor of his helmet is closed, you cannot see his face at all.

Plate armour was heavy. It was also difficult to move about in.

German Gothic armour for riding (about 1480)

Helmets became more highly decorated. The small picture (left) shows part of a statue on a knight's tomb. His head is resting on a helmet with a swan's head crest.

The painting below is by the Italian artist Uccello. It shows armoured knights in battle.

Jousting

Knights needed to practice their skills just as sportsmen do now. The rider in the picture (right) is learning to fight on horseback. He is trying to hit the shield without being knocked from his horse. This was called 'tilting at the quintain'.

sandbag quintain

A contest in which knights fought against each other for fun was called a tournament. Jousting was a contest between two mounted knights armed with lances.

Knights were sometimes killed in tournaments.

Decoration

The best armour was made to fit the person who was going to wear it. A locksmith fitted the hinges, straps, buckles and hooks to fasten it. Often, armour was beautifully decorated. The painting opposite shows Sir Henry Hastings in full armour.

Breastplate (Italy)

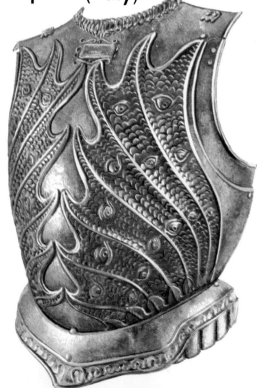

Gauntlet (Italy)

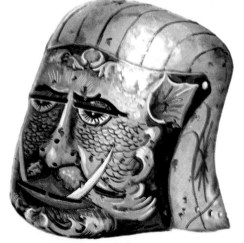

Painted helmet (Germany)

A·DÑI·1·5·8·8
ÆTATIS·SVÆ·52

Animal Armour

Armour became so heavy that a knight could hardly move without his horse. It was therefore important that his horse was not killed. So horses were given armour too. The special saddle helped to prevent the knight being knocked off his horse.

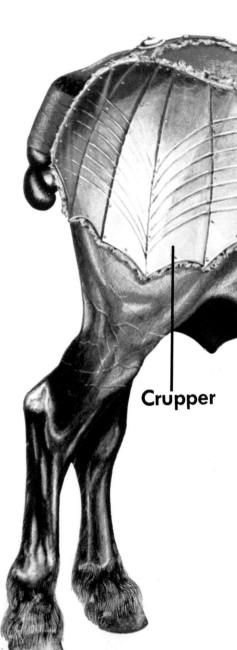

Crupper

Even elephants sometimes had armour. This suit of elephant armour came from India. The dog may have been used to carry messages on the battlefield.

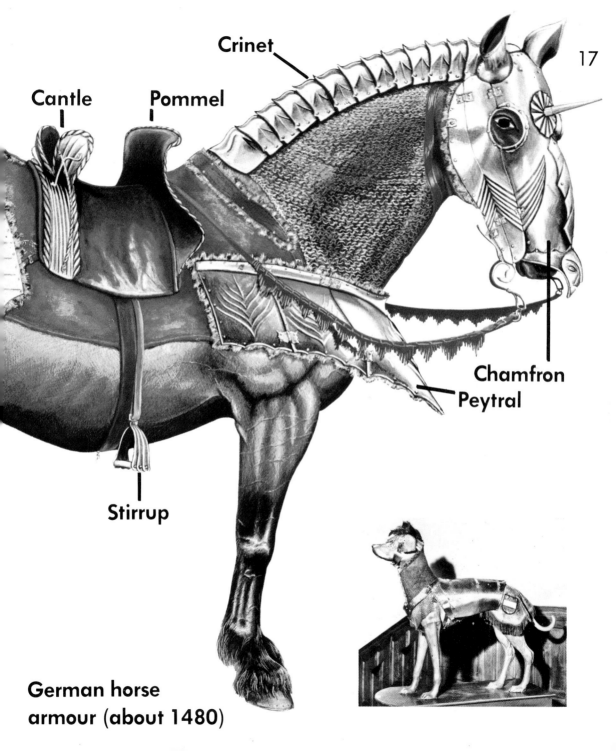

Crinet

Cantle

Pommel

Chamfron

Peytral

Stirrup

German horse
armour (about 1480)

Eastern Armour

This highly decorated Turkish helmet (right) has been made in the shape of a turban. It has a sliding noseguard.

Indian armour

On the left is a suit of Indian armour. It is mostly made of thick cloth. A complete suit of plate armour would have got much too hot under the Indian sun.

Here is a Japanese knight
(*samurai*) on horseback.

Modern Armour

Fighting in the English Civil War

Armour was not much use against guns. As guns became more accurate, men wore less armour. Three hundred years ago, many soldiers just wore breastplates.

In both World Wars, soldiers used helmets to protect their heads. Today, troops wear bullet-proof vests called flak jackets.

Modern flak jackets

**Helmet and face mask
(World War I)**

Glossary

Armour   Any covering that protects a man in battle.

Breastplate   A piece of armour to protect the chest and stomach.

Bronze   A metal made by mixing together copper and tin.

Crest   A plume or figure on top of a helmet.

Gladiator   A professional fighter in Roman times.

Lance   A kind of spear used by knights.

Locksmith   A person who makes and repairs locks and fastenings.

Mail Armour   Armour made of hundreds of small metal rings. It is also called chain mail.

Plate Armour   Armour made of plates of metal joined together.

Quintain   A post with a weighted cross-piece which enabled a knight to practise jousting.

Tapestry   A piece of material with a design embroidered on it.

Trident   A spear with three prongs.

Turban   A head-dress consisting of a sash or scarf wound round the head.

Visor   The front part of a helmet that protects the face and eyes.

2 3 4 5 6 7 8 9 10— R —85 84 83 82